Mr. Nobody

By
Kerstin Fletcher
(& Family)

Special thanks to Judy Morgan, Elizabeth Olah, and Jen Hunt.

Copyright © 2015, Santa Rosa, CA.
All Rights Reserved.
ISBN 978-0-9891660-3-4

This book is dedicated to
my Mr. Nobodies:
Carl, Johanna, Magdeline,
Lilyana, and Carl.
You all helped so much
with this story!

I love you all!

There's an invisible creature we can't see,

We believe he goes by "Mr. Nobody."

Mr. Nobody may be his simple name,

But he drives parents completely insane.

We don't spot his person anywhere,

Just see what he's done here and there.

When Mama searches for scissors or tape,

All four of us children run to escape.

"We did not take them," say Carl and Lily,

While Maggie and Hanna quickly agree.

No scissors or tape far as eyes can see—

Must have been that Mr. Nobody!

From the bathroom comes Papa's stern yell.

"No toilet paper again?!"—we know that tone well.

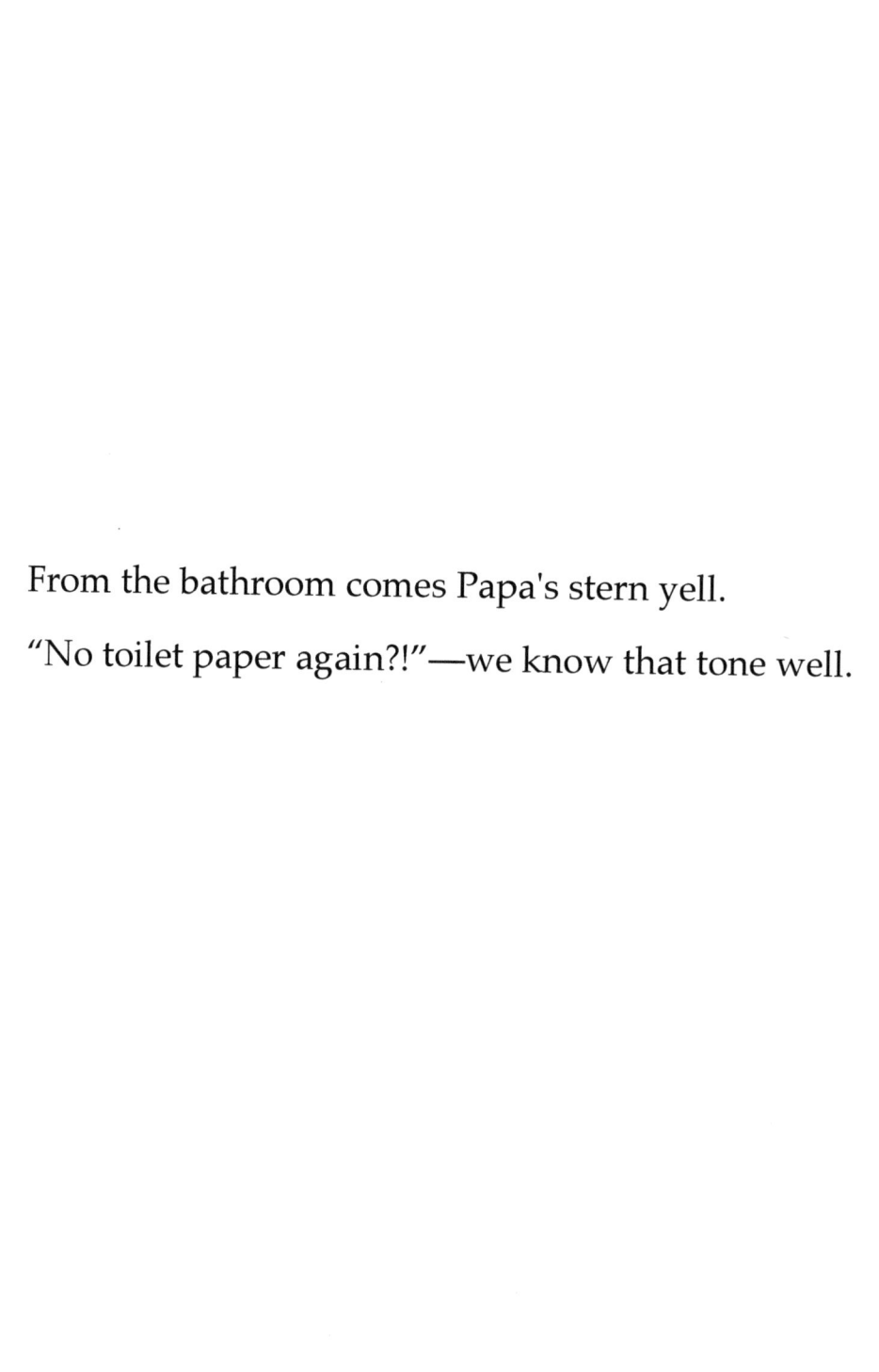

The empty roll waving, more proof to see,

Once again we've been struck by Mr. Nobody.

Mama bakes chocolate chip cookies at lunch,

For Papa, and all of us children to munch.

The next day comes and we'd like to eat more,

With the ice cold milk Hanna will eagerly pour.

What a shock! Oh unhappy surprise!

Only a trace of crumbs meets our eyes!

"We did not take them," say Lily and Carl.

While Hanna and Maggie echo their call.

We all exclaim, "It wasn't me!"

It *has* to be...Mr. Nobody.

The dishes are done, the kitchen is clean.

No unwashed cups or platters are seen.

But the next moment a huge pile does appear.

"From where?" asks Maggie. "It's so unclear."

Our shoes and socks are left lying around,

But how they got there has Lily dumbfound.

Cupboard doors open, bathroom floors wet,

Papa asks, "Who was the one to forget?"

As we grow up, less "mysteries" abound.

Seems Mr. Nobody has not stuck around.

More and more is in place every day.

Where he went, we cannot say.

Is it possible that he's moved away,

Only to pop up at YOUR house some day?

The End

Or is it...?